In Their Pain

Great Women

of

the Bible

ERIKA GREY

Pedante Press

Advice for Life in These End Times Series

All Scriptural quotations in this publication are from the New King James Version of the Bible © by Thomas Nelson, Inc.

Printed in the United States of America

Copyright © 2021 Erika Grey

All rights reserved.

ISBN: 978-1-940844-26-8

DEDICATION

To you, my readers

CONTENTS

	Acknowledgments	i
1	My Story	1
2	No Comfort	4
3	Naomi and Ruth	17
4	Barrenness- Sarah	25
5	Other Childless Women	31
6	The Shunammite Woman	44
7	Tragic Lives-Leah & Rachel	53
8	More Women Who Suffered	61
9	On Suffering-Jesus	69
10	Jesus Said To Endure	74

www.erikagrey.com

For Bible Prophecy news and analysis and more from the Advice for Living in These End times Series visit my website.

1 MY STORY

At times, the unbearable pain and sadness crushes me like a grape in the winepress. My life's events have broken me into minute fragmented pieces. Emotionally I am destroyed. If I think on Jesus and my mission for Him my pain abates.

Peter Sinking When He Loses Sight of Jesus

This is the lesson taught in Matthew 14:22-33. In the story the apostle Peter is out in a boat in the middle of a windy storm at night. Jesus came to them walking on the water. Peter asked if he could also walk on water and he was able to if he looked at Jesus, but the minute he fixated on the high winds he began to sink.

Like Peter, if I gaze at Jesus I do not sink and for me it is into the flooding waters of my grief. For the most part I meditate on Jesus and my mission for Him and go forward with my work. I deliberately avoid my triggers: the environments that bring up my pain.

One day while coming home from church and looking over my life and all my losses which are numerous, I wondered if other women in ministry have experienced the level of hardships as myself.

My Life of Many Losses

Some of the episodes of my life are so unbelievable that they replay out of a wild cinematic film. No one can imagine. Becoming a Christian did not guarantee me a better life, on the contrary my unsaved family members enjoyed those. I once attributed the events to my having been a lukewarm Christian with God literally breaking me to draw me closer. But as I sold out and put Jesus first, and embarked on my ministry, I would enter the worst decade of my life.

It seems my entire life has been characterized by loss. Many of the things that people are given in this life or take for granted have not been a part of mine. If that were all not enough, in a two-year period I experienced six deaths, two years later I would experience four more. The world I lived in changed forever. The losses did not just come from the deaths, but in other areas and many of them. As a result, on certain days my prevailing mood is one of sadness.

The Women of the Bible

It was during one of my grief-stricken moments that I realized that nearly all women of the Bible had an area of pain. That it was in their despair that God used them as God was now using me in mine.

2 NO COMFORT

There is a prevalent teaching in the church that a Christian is supposed to be happy all the time. That in Christ we find joy despite our circumstances.

If you are not rejoicing, you are not living your Christian life right; you are sinning. Leaders site the story of the apostles singing and praising in prison and the door opening to free them. Yes, there is a time for praise and when God does miraculously reverse our circumstances. If someone is suddenly widowed or loses a loved one, this cannot be turned around. Evangelical Christian churches emphasize that in Christ you can achieve a pain free life if you are walking in the Spirit. The fruit of the Spirit is joy, not sadness. Just as happiness does not affect our joy in the spirit, neither does sadness. One can be grateful for their salvation and what God has done in their life but still suffer grief.

Lovers of Pleasure

The idea of a pain free life is not only aimed for in Evangelical Christian circles but also in the world. Doctors have a pill for every kind of mental anguish you might suffer. This explains why drug addiction has increased significantly along with obesity. People expect to feel good all the time. Unknowingly they become lovers of pleasure more than lovers of God. The proof is in the rise of the various addictions.

2 Timothy 3:1-5 tells us that in the last days people will be lovers of pleasure more than lovers of God. This sinful pursuit has even reached into the Church. They treat Jesus and the Spirit like they are feel good pills to make you feel better and take you out of your grief or sadness.

Pain is a Part of Life

When I was giving birth to my youngest, I

had a home birth with a midwife. On the discomfort of labor, she said that there is this idea that all pain should be eliminated. When pain is a part of life. It is the same with emotional distress. Not only should we not eliminate it, but sometimes there is just no comfort or consolation for the afflictions we suffer.

The Bible Recognizes Our Pain

Unlike what is taught by pastors of churches the Bible recognizes pain that has lasting and devastating effects in one's life. We see this in the life of Isaac who lost his mother Sarah. According to Jewish Rabbi's he was 37 years old when she died. Three years later he married Rebecca. The Bible states that after getting married, Isaac was comforted after his mother's death. Genesis 24:67 reads:

"Then Isaac brought her into his mother Sarah's tent; and he took Rebekah, and she became his wife, and he loved her. So, Isaac was comforted after his mother's death."

Here the Scriptures recognize Isaac's grief three years after losing his mother. God provided a wife as a consolation. In this passage the Bible recognizes loss as having a lingering impact.

Times of No Comfort in Bible

There are also the times of no comfort. We see this in Jeremiah 31:15. This was a prophecy that was fulfilled with the killing of the firstborn boys in Jerusalem by Herod. After he had been informed by the wise men of the birth of Christ, which he interpreted as a king that would replace him, he issued the decree. The verse predicted and was fulfilled:

"Thus says the LORD, "A voice is heard in Ramah, Lamentation and bitter weeping. Rachel is weeping for her children; She refuses to be comforted because they are no more."

Yes, the loss of a child, for which there is no consolation. This is true, after loss one feels completely shattered. I remember going to church and telling someone how sad and depressed I was over all my recent losses. This individual told me that I should go on an antidepressant. I stated, "For what, I am feeling exactly how I should be feeling." In part the purpose of this book is to let you know that if you are feeling sad because you have suffered loss, trauma, or any other misfortune, don't let anyone tell you that you should feel otherwise.

The Grief of Widowhood

The first chapter of the book of Lamentations talks about the desolation of Israel by the Babylonians. The Scriptures compare widowhood and the loss of a mate as the desolation left after the Babylonian army destroyed and ransacked Judah and carried off its inhabitants.

It compares the nation's emotional state to the grief of widowhood and the despair of slavery. Lamentations 1: 1-4records:

How lonely sits the city, That was full of people! How like a widow is she, Who was great among the nations! The princess among the provinces Has become a slave.
She weeps bitterly in the night, Her tears are on her cheeks; Among all her lovers She has none to comfort her. All her friends have dealt treacherously with her; They have become her enemies.
Judah as gone into captivity, Under affliction and hard servitude; She dwells among the nations, She finds no rest; All her persecutors overtake her in dire straits.
The roads to Zion mourn

Because no one comes to the set feasts.
All her gates are desolate; Her priests sigh, Her virgins are afflicted, And she is in bitterness.

Yet not only are widows completely disregarded and ignored in today's churches, but she is expected to bounce right back emotionally because she has Christ. God recognizes the widow's pain.

Tamar's Rape and Resulting Desolation

In 2 Samuel 13, we see a picture of bereavement and destitution in the life of Tamar, King David's daughter. In the story she is raped by her half-brother Amnon who had fallen in love with her. As he is beginning to force her into the act, she tells him that if he speaks to the king, he will give her to him as a wife. Emotionally she can deal with her father arranging a marriage and becoming his wife.

He refused to listen to her, raped her and afterwards hated her as much as he had loved her. The king's virgin daughters wore robes of many colors identifying them. Samuel 13:19 records, *"Then Tamar put ashes on her head and tore her robe of many colors that was on her and laid her hand on her head and went away crying bitterly."*

Verse 20 tells us the sad result, *"So Tamar remained desolate in her brother Absalom's house."* The word used for desolate in the original Hebrew regarding a person means destroyed.

Shame from Rape

Many have interpreted that this rape destroyed Tamar because virginity was required for marriage. Theologians totally disregard that Tamar's desolation also included the destruction from the act of the rape itself. Notice she also said to her brother, *"No, my brother, do not force me, for no such thing should be done in Israel. Do not do this disgraceful thing! And I, where could I take my shame?*

The shame or reproach would come from having been raped. Rape is a violent act, and more so, it treats the victim as an object. During a rape the victim is both degraded and controlled by the perpetrator. The shame or reproach is the scar the victim remains with after the rape. If it occurs during one's virginity, the first sexual experience occurring in a love relationship is robbed from the victim and provides a significant loss and distortion of the sexual act. Emotionally` the rape victim is left desolate meaning broken.

According to Strong's, the reproach is the same as widowhood. Isaiah 54:4, *"the reproach of widowhood,"* i.e., which rests on widows. Figuratively a person or thing which is despised. It rests on a condition of shame or disgrace.

God Relates Shame of Rape to Widowhood?

Whenever anyone suffers the loss of spouse, there is the underlying feeling of shame. Why me? Why do other couples live together into real old age and I lost mine? Why am I now alone? Deep down is the feeling that something is wrong with you for this to have happened to you. It is also the same with rape. It elicits the same feelings and effects a woman's view of herself as having any value. The Bible is an amazing book as it reveals the depths of men and women's psychology.

Two Types of Widows

There are two types of widows; those who married, and their husband's died to women who never married. This brings us to our next story of devastation and loss, the story of Jephthah's daughter. Jephthah was a judge of

Israel who defeated the Ammonites. He made a vow to God. If He gave Jephthah victory in the battle against, the Ammonites, he would offer whatever came out of his doors of his house to meet him as a burnt offering. Jephthah is mentioned in Hebrews 11:32, the Bible's hall of faith. These offerings were voluntary and made my men who represented their family. They were given in conjunction with another sacrifice.

According to Judges this was Jephthah's only child. To his horror, she came out to greet her father with timbrels and dancing.

Judges 11:35-40 reads:

^{35} And it came to pass, when he saw her, that he tore his clothes, and said, "Alas, my daughter! You have brought me very low! You are among those who trouble me! For I have given my word to the LORD, and I cannot go back on it."

^{36} So she said to him, "My father, if you have given your word to the LORD, do to me according to what has gone out of your mouth, because the LORD has avenged you of your enemies, the people of Ammon." ^{37} Then she said to her father, "Let this thing be done for me: let me alone for two months, that

I may go and wander on the mountains and bewail my virginity, my friends and I."

³⁸ So he said, "Go." And he sent her away for two months; and she went with her friends and bewailed her virginity on the mountains. ³⁹ And it was so at the end of two months that she returned to her father, and he carried out his vow with her which he had vowed. She knew no man.

And it became a custom in Israel ⁴⁰ that the daughters of Israel went four days each year to lament the daughter of Jephthah the Gileadite.

Jephthah essentially offered his daughter to the service of God.

Bewail in the Hebrew means mourn, weep, make lamentation. Jephthah's daughter's loss came by something that she will never have in this life. Something that many others have and take for granted.

Widowhood

The story of the birth of Ichabod in 1 Samuel 4 records when the Ark of the Covenant was captured by the Philistines. Just as Eli's daughter in law was about to give birth, she heard the news that her husband and father-in-law were dead, and that the Ark had been captured. 1 Samuel 4: 20-22 records:

[20] And about the time of her death the women who stood by her said to her, "Do not fear, for you have borne a son." But she did not answer, nor did she regard it. [21] Then she named the child Ichabod, saying, "The glory has departed from Israel!" because the ark of God had been captured and because of her father-in-law and her husband. [22] And she said, "The glory has departed from Israel, for the ark of God has been captured."

The grief for Eli's pregnant daughter in law was so great from the loss of the Ark of God and her father-in-law and husband's death, that it brought on her labor. She named her child Ichabod. In addition, she was in such a state of shock and grief she could not even hear her son's birth announcement let alone rejoice in it. She died moments after, either by injury or by giving birth.

Jesus Wept

In the New Testament, we see Martha weeping over Lazarus, and it is the only place in the Bible that records that Jesus wept.

Afterwards Jesus raised Lazarus from the dead. Did Jesus say you have Me, so you should not be crying? Not at all, God clearly understands our suffering and that sadly it is a part of this life. In addition, there is pain for which there is no comfort. There is no one who should tell you that you are doing something wrong in the spirit because you feel sadness from loss. Neither should anyone tell you that your grief should be over in a certain time frame. Many wounds last a lifetime. If it were not so God would not promise in Revelation 21:4:

"And God will wipe away every tear from their eyes; there shall be no more death, nor sorrow, nor crying. There shall be no more pain, for the former things have passed away."

If in Christ, we could eliminate our affliction that verse would not have been written. Rather, Jesus comes alongside us in our suffering.

Great Women of the Bible Hurt Emotionally

We see an interesting pattern in Scripture, the great women of the Bible, nearly all of them suffered some great burden, tragedy, or loss. While their pain does not go away, we see answers to their prayers. In some miracles happen and in others, God provides a restoration, or a consolation as they remain faithful to Him.

3 NAOMI AND RUTH

The book of Ruth tells the story of a woman by the name of Naomi who experiences unprecedented tragedy and loss. The first chapter of the book tells her story. She first loses her husband and after he dies each of her son's die. Her two daughters-in-law remain. These losses occurred over a ten-year period. If this were not enough, a famine strikes the land. Not only does Naomi experience the loss of her husband and children, but no doubt, the famine would only have seared like a hot iron into her flesh the pain of her loss as her husband and sons would have been able to obtain food.

What also becomes clear in the story is that

Naomi has a solid walk with God. Her faith is evident in her actions, and her words. In addition, she is a walking testimony to her daughter in laws.

Naomi Steps Out in Faith

Naomi was living in Moab at this time and verse six records that she heard there that *"the Lord had visited His people by giving them bread."* This verse provides a view into Ruth's faith and that she saw God as the source of sustenance. She viewed Him as providing in this time of famine. In an act of faith, she would go where God was blessing and to reunite with the faithful or her people in Judah.

God Foremost in Naomi's Mind

Another statement evidencing Naomi's faith occurs as she is telling her daughter in laws goodbye and wishing them well. She states: *"May God treat you as kindly as you treated me and your husbands."* Again, God is foremost in her mind. She hopes that He will reward her daughter in laws for their kindness to her sons, their husbands. She tells them to go back to their households that they might meet another husband. She again states in verse 13, *"it grieves me very much for your sakes that the hand of the Lord has gone out against me."* Naomi recognizes that it was God's hand in the death of her husband and sons. While she is not happy about it, she does not curse God.

Naomi's Restoration

In the next passage we see Naomi's first restoration by God, her daughter in law Ruth has become like a daughter.

¹⁶ But Ruth said:

*"Entreat[c] me not to leave you,
Or to turn back from following after you;
For wherever you go, I will go;
And wherever you lodge, I will lodge;
Your people shall be my people,
And your God, my God.
¹⁷ Where you die, I will die,
And there will I be buried.
The LORD do so to me, and more also,
If anything but death parts you and me."*

Naomi's other daughter in law goes back to her home, but Ruth clings to her. Both are widows. Not only does Ruth attach herself to Naomi because of her godly love towards Ruth but also Naomi's walk is a testimony for Ruth, and she wants her same God. It is the testimony of Naomi that wins Ruth to the God of Israel.

Naomi's Sorrow

Did Naomi exhibit joy? On the contrary. In the next verse they arrive at Bethlehem and everyone who knew Naomi is happy to see her. Naomi's response relays the depth of her sadness. The passage records:

¹⁹ Now the two of them went until they came to Bethlehem. And it happened, when they had come to Bethlehem, that all the city was excited because of them; and the women said, "Is this Naomi?" ²⁰ But she said to them, "Do not call me Naomi; call me Mara, for the Almighty has dealt very bitterly with me. ²¹ I went out full, and the LORD has brought me home again empty. Why do you call me Naomi, since the LORD has testified against me, and the Almighty has afflicted me?"

Bitterness

Naomi changed her name to bitterness whereas Naomi means my delight, pleasantness. She was bitter over what had happened to her and yet she remained faithful to God and accepted his harsh hand her life. Ruth witnessed her sadness, grief, despair, and her unwavering faith. Some think that faith is always hoping for the situation to improve. When having faith also means accepting a situation for what it is and still obeying God.

Ecclesiastes 3: 1-8 states *there is a time for everything….A time to cry and a time to laugh, A time to grieve and a time to dance."* Ruth was bitter and sad and rightfully so, she lost her husband and her two sons. She also looked forward to her sons and daughter in laws having grandchildren. This was another loss.

Boaz-Kinsman Redeemer

As the story unfolds the barley harvest started and Ruth went to work in the field. She ended up in Boaz's land, an extremely wealthy relative of Naomi's husband. He favored her because he heard how she left her family, people and land of her birth to be with Naomi and her God, the Lord God of Israel. Boaz instructed extra provision for Ruth.

When Naomi learned Ruth gleaned in Boaz's field. Ruth 2:20 records, *"Then Naomi said to her daughter-in-law, "Blessed be the LORD, who has not forsaken His kindness to the living and the dead!" And Naomi said to her, "This man is a relation of ours, one of our close relatives.* This is a powerful statement by Naomi, that God even grants the wishes of those who are now deceased after they die.

The Request

In Jewish law a brother could marry the widow of his brother and carry on the family name through the offspring. Naomi instructed Ruth on what to do and how to approach Boaz in this matter and make the request. This was Boaz's response:

¹⁰ Then he said, "Blessed are you of the LORD, my daughter! For you have shown more kindness at the end than at the beginning, in that you did not go after young men, whether poor or rich. ¹¹ And now, my daughter, do not fear. I will do for you all that you request, for all the people of my town know that you are a virtuous woman. ¹² Now it is true that I am a close relative; however, there is a relative closer than I. ¹³ Stay this night, and in the morning, it shall be that if he will perform the duty of a close relative for you—good; let him do it. But if he does not want to perform the duty for you, then I will perform the duty for you, as the LORD lives! Lie down until morning."

Boaz gave Ruth food to bring to her mother-in-law. Naomi told Ruth that Boaz would conclude the matter this day and he did. The other man declined, and Boaz made it clear to the elders that he would take her to be his wife. They married and Ruth conceived and bore a son.

Naomi's Restoration from God

Then came the restoration. The women of Judah told Naomi that her daughter in law who loves her is better than seven sons. Naomi placed her son on Ruth's bosom, and she became a nurse to him. In addition, the child was the grandfather of King David, whose line would continue to the birth of Christ. The Scripture records:

³ So Boaz took Ruth and she became his wife; and when he went in to her, the LORD gave her conception, and she bore a son. ¹⁴ Then the women said to Naomi, "Blessed be the LORD, who has not left you this day without a close relative; and may his name be famous in Israel! ¹⁵ And may he be to you a restorer of life and a nourisher of your old age; for your daughter-in-law, who loves you, who is better to you than seven sons, has borne him." ¹⁶ Then Naomi took the child and laid him on her bosom, and became a nurse to him. ¹⁷ Also the neighbor women gave him a name, saying, "There is a son born to Naomi." And they called his name Obed. He is the father of Jesse, the father of David.:

Ruth lost her husband and two sons, and nothing could ever replace them. God gave her instead a special relationship with her daughter in law. This grew strong as they shared their loss of their husbands. In addition to Ruth witnessing Naomi's faith. Naomi got her grandchild, this she never expected. Only this child would be the grandfather of David, a king of Israel and would also be in the line of Christ. We see in the Bible that God uses the brokenhearted, the desolate in this life for great tasks. In addition, He is the God of the impossible.

4 BARRENESS-SARAH

One of the first situations we see in Scripture as a source of emotional pain for women is having a barren womb. These women desired children but were unable to have them. In ancient society the inability to bear children marked a woman as if she had leprosy. In some societies the women were regarded as outcasts. For those who have been blessed with little ones, they cannot imagine the suffering of a woman who desires a baby and is barren, let alone if she lived in ancient society.

Womb Raiders

One cannot imagine the sense of loss these women feel when they see children playing or mothers with their newborns. So great is this desire for many women that there are "womb raiders." These include those who steel babies or even kill a pregnant mother and cut the infant from the womb to claim it as their own. Fetus theft became a relatively new category of crime in the United States. The first reported case was documented in 1974.

Concubines, Handmaids & Fertility Treatments

Fertility treatments in the world are big business with couples spending thousands of dollars to have a baby. Couples have spent upwards of 70,000 US dollars to conceive. In the Bible, the method used to have children for the barren was the use of concubines or handmaids. These women would bear children for another becoming an additional wife so to speak. In the Bible, kings often had concubines. Their status was inferior to a wife.

Emotional Trauma from Barrenness

The inability to conceive takes a major toll on a woman. Regina Townsend founder of "The Broken Brown Egg," an infertility website wrote in the New York Times, *The*

Lasting Trauma of Infertility "How many people do we pass every single day who are carrying around raging fires—who have a passion or a pain inside that is so great they can barely contain it? For me, and for thousands of other people, infertility is that raging fire.

In her article she talks about the level of depression and anxiety and living between despair and hope. Moreover, when she did finally have a child through the laborious process of IVF and a C-section, she lived as one who experienced trauma, waiting for the other shoe to drop. Loss does this, it leaves the individual scarred. We even see this in a couple of the cases of the barren women of the Bible once they conceive.

The Church's Lack of Empathy

Sadly, the barren woman in the church might not receive empathy. She will be told that Jesus is enough to satisfy her desire. If she grows despondent or discouraged, they will add insult to injury by telling her that she is not living her Christian life to the fullest. It is men and women who have children that will admonish her.

The reality is that Jesus just cannot meet that desire. He cannot become the baby that is hers, that she delivers and can hold and raise and watch grow. God in fact understands her pain. When she looks to Him, He will provide a restoration. In addition, God performs His biggest miracles in the lives of the broken from loss. God and Jesus understand that which the church does not comprehend or even live up to in their own lives.

Sarah

Abraham's wife Sarah was both a beautiful woman and childless. She went her entire life barren. She did not conceive until she was 90 years old. Genesis 17 and 18 record the account. When she learned she would get pregnant and bear a son she laughed. Genesis 18:13 states,

"And the Lord said to Abraham, "Why did Sarah laugh, saying, 'Shall I surely bear a child, since I am old?' Is anything too hard for the Lord? At the appointed time I shall return to you and Sarah shall have a son."

Sarah would have Isaac and because she was old when she had him, she would die while he was still young. The Bible gives evidence that Sarah died before her son Isaac married. Genesis 24:67 records:

⁶⁷Then Isaac brought her into his mother Sarah's tent; and he took Rebekah and she became his wife, and he loved her. So Isaac was comforted after his mother's death.

Isaac had suffered the loss of his mother and we see even in his life, God providing a wife to act as a comfort for him after his mother's death. God would also show Himself that He is the God of miracles. When he provides a restoration for loss it is usually miraculous.

While Sarah would suffer nearly her entire life being childless, she would in her old age bear a son. She must have also known that she would not see her son marry or hold her grandchildren. No doubt this must have also been painful for her. She most likely suffered increased anxiety and been overprotective of Isaac because of her suffering. Yet Sarah became the mother of many nations. She is the great grandmother of the forefathers of Israel. She also exists in the bloodline of Jesus. In addition, she was written in Hebrews Hall of

Faith for believing God despite years of her inability to bear children. This equates to loss and not having those things in life that most take for granted, such as children or a marriage.

God even changed Sarah's name from Sarai meaning princess with the suggestion of being quarrelsome. A similar name today is when a woman is called a prima donna. God named her Sarah, which means noblewoman. A woman of high rank. Imagine that the woman who became the mother of the Jewish nation was barren for most of her life. God is the God of the impossible. In addition, he uses broken women for great tasks and for the display of his miracles.

5 OTHER CHILDLESS WOMEN

Hannah could not have a baby. Her husband's other wife Peninnah had children and would torment her and deliberately make her jealous. Yet Hannah had the love of her husband more than Peninnah. The Bible records the story in 1 Samuel Chapter 1.

Now there was a certain man of Ramathaim Zophim, of the mountains of Ephraim, and his name was Elkanah the son of Jeroham, the son of Elihu, the son of Tohu, the son of Zuph, an Ephraimite. ² And he had two wives: the name of one was Hannah, and the name of the other Peninnah. Peninnah had children, but Hannah had no children. ³ This man went up from his city yearly to worship and sacrifice to the LORD of hosts in Shiloh.

Also the two sons of Eli, Hophni and Phinehas, the priests of the LORD, were there. ⁴And whenever the time came for Elkanah to make an offering, he would give portions to Peninnah his wife and to all her sons and daughters. ⁵But to Hannah he would give a double portion, for he loved Hannah, although the LORD had closed her womb. ⁶And her rival also provoked her severely, to make her miserable, because the LORD had closed her womb. ⁷So it was, year by year, when she went up to the house of the LORD, that she provoked her; therefore she wept and did not eat.

Hannah Prays

Although Hannah had an incredibly loving relationship with her husband, this was not enough. She wanted a child. She went to the Temple and prayed. While pouring out her heart, soul, and prayers Eli the priest overheard her. He thought she was drunk. She promised the Lord that if He would give her a son, she would give him back to God and consecrate him to the Lord with the Nazarite vow. In this she would never cut his hair.

God Answers Hannah's Prayer

God answered Hannah's prayer and gave her a son. She named him Samuel, meaning heard of God. She nursed him. When he was weaned, she brought him to the Temple. She handed him to the care of Eli the priest. 1 Samuel 1: 27-28 records that Hannah stated:

"For this child I prayed, and the Lord has granted me my petition which I asked of Him. Therefore I also have lent him to the Lord; as long as he lives he shall be lent to the Lord.

Afterwards she sang a song and referenced barrenness. In 1 Samuel 2:5 she sings: *"Those who were full have hired themselves out for bread, And the hungry have ceased to hunger. Even the barren has borne seven, And she who has many children has become feeble."*

Hannah Loans Her Son to the Lord

As a child the Bible tells us in 1 Samuel 2:18 that Samuel ministered unto the Lord wearing a linen ephod. Hannah each year made him a little robe. She brought him a new one each year when she went to the Temple with her husband to offer the yearly sacrifice. Eli blessed her and her husband for the loan they gave to the Lord and asked for more children for her.

God Blesses Hannah With More Children

In verse 21 the Bible tells us that "the Lord visited Hannah, so that she conceived and bore three sons and two daughters. Meanwhile the child Samuel grew before the Lord. Not only did Hannah receive from God a restoration, but Samuel went onto become one of God's prophets. He prophesized during the reign of Saul, the first king of Israel.

In Hannah's barrenness and grief, she remained close to God. This was revealed by her giving this child back to the Lord and completing her vow. In addition, because of her walk with God, her child Samuel had the power of God on his life. Samuel was raised under the tutelage of Eli, whose grievous sin of putting his evil sons before God brought judgement onto him and his sons. It was not an ideal spiritual environment. Yet Samuel grew in favor with God and man because of the solid walk of his mother.

Monah's Wife- The Mother of Sampson

Judges chapter 13 records the story of the birth of Sampson. His father's name was Zorah of the tribe of Dan. The Bible tells us that "*his wife was barren and had no children.*" An angel of the Lord appeared to his wife and said, *"indeed now you are barren and have borne no children, but you shall conceive and bear a son."*

In addition, the angel of the Lord told her that he should not be given wine and no razor shall come upon his head, meaning he was to be a Nazarite to God from the womb. The same as the prophet and judge Samuel. And that he would deliver Israel out of the hand of the Philistines, "Judges 13: 4-5 records that she goes to her husband and tells him,

"A Man of God came to me, and His countenance was like the countenance of the Angel of God, very awesome; but I did not ask Him where He was from, and He did not tell me His name. ⁷And He said to me, 'Behold, you shall conceive and bear a son. Now drink no wine or similar drink, nor eat anything unclean, for the child shall be a Nazirite to God from the womb to the day of his death."

This means Sampson will be consecrated to God. What is noteworthy here is that Sampson's mother was to live as a Nazarite and not even drink wine while the child was in her womb. We know that the mother's blood flows through the fetus and sustains it. What the mother eats passes to the baby. This was later discovered by doctors.

Then Manoah prayed to God and asked if the Man of God who He sent could come again and teach he and his wife what they should do for the child. The Bible says that the Lord listened to Manoah and the Angel of God came to the woman again as she was sitting in a field. Manoah was not with her. She ran to her husband and told him that the Man who appeared the other day just came to her again. The Scriptures states:

"So Manoah arose and followed his wife. When he came to the Man, he said to Him, "Are the Man who spoke to this woman?" And He said, I am."

Menoah said, *"Now let Your words come to pass! What will the boy's rule of life, and his work?*

Essentially this is what the Man of God relayed to the woman, his rules for his life and what God would have him to do. The Man of God reiterated what he told his wife to Manoah.

Manoah asked Him to stay because they prepared a goat offering for him. He answered and said, *"thou you are detaining me I will not eat of your bread but if you make an offering you are to make it to the Lord."*

Manoah asked the man his name. He basically answered, *"Why do you ask my name seeing it is wonderful."* While the NKJV of the Bible translates His answer as wonderful the KJV renders the word as secret. The Hebrew word piliy, means wonderful, incompressible. and extraordinary. Theologians agree that the Man of God, Angel of the Lord appearances in the Old Testament is God sending His own Son.

Manoah took the goat with a meat offering and offered it on a rock to the Lord. As he and his wife were looking just as the flame rose on the altar, the angel of the Lord ascended in the flame on the altar. When Manoah and his wife witnessed this, they fell on their faces to the ground. It was at that moment they knew this was an Angel of the Lord. Manoah thought that because they had seen the Lord, they would die.

Manoah's wife stated that if the Lord wanted to kill them, He would not have received their burnt offering and meat offering, and neither would He have revealed to them all he told them. The Scripture records that the next year they had a son and named him Samson and the Lord blessed him.

We see a pattern that these women who are completely broken and saddened by barrenness, yet who are faithful to God receive the child they longed for and for great purposes of God. You may ask, what extraordinary purpose did Samson have in killing the Philistines that Christ would appear?

The Philistines were remnants of the giants, these were the half man half demon race that Satan ushered into the world to subvert God's plan. The story of the Nephilim goes to the core of the battle of the ages. They also represent a Christian's greatest battles. Victory is always achieved via obedience to God and reliance on Him.

Elizabeth

Luke 1: 5-23 records the story of Elizabeth Mary's cousin who suffered from being barren. In addition to Sarah, she is also old as is her husband. She is from the line of the Levites or Priests. The Bible tells us she is a daughter of

Aaron. Her husband Zacharias is a priest at the time of Herod in Judea. As Zacharias is serving God in the temple, burning incense and was alone, an angel appeared to him. As the angel appeared on the right side of the alter of incense, fear enveloped Zacharias. The Bible records:

13 But the angel said to him, "Do not be afraid, Zacharias, for your prayer is heard; and your wife Elizabeth will bear you a son, and you shall call his name John. 14 And you will have joy and gladness, and many will rejoice at his birth. 15 For he will be great in the sight of the Lord and shall drink neither wine nor strong drink. He will also be filled with the Holy Spirit, even from his mother's womb. 16 And he will turn many of the children of Israel to the Lord their God. 17 He will also go before Him in the spirit and power of Elijah, 'to turn the hearts of the fathers to the children,' and the disobedient to the wisdom of the just, to make ready a people prepared for the Lord."

Zacharias' Unbelief

18 And Zacharias said to the angel, "How shall I know this? For I am an old man, and my wife is well advanced in years."

Essentially, Zacharias was asking how it is

possible for him to have sexual relations as well Elizabeth having a baby. Zacharias did not believe. The angel Gabrielle told him that he would be dumb, and not able to speak until the child was born because of his unbelief.

God's Restoration for Elizabeth

We see in the life of Elizabeth another restoration for the loss of her ability to bear children. Again, this becomes the way that God choses to usher in a mighty prophet. The Bible records that Elizabeth upon becoming pregnant then hid herself. This has baffled Bible teachers because this is not the expected response to her discovering she is having a baby. In Elizabeth's old age this might have been a way for her to pamper herself during her pregnancy, she might have known that her age would present more risks. She was now doing her part for the best for her child.

More Shame

We see again the topic of shame brought up that we saw first with Tamar's rape, and with widowhood. Now we see it with a woman being barren.

Elizabeth stated, *"Thus hath the Lord dealt with me in the days wherein he looked on me, to take away my reproach among men."* Reproach is another word for shame. In a society where most women are having children, and barren women are considered outcasts she feels shame. Barrenness would have been considered like a defect in her person. It also singles her out from among the mothers with children.

God of the Impossible

When the angel Gabriel announces to Mary her supernatural conception, he reiterates God's miracle for Elizabeth. Gabriel states:

[36] *"And, behold, thy cousin Elisabeth, she hath also conceived a son in her old age: and this is the sixth month with her, who was called barren."*

[37] *For with God nothing shall be impossible.*

Mary was a virgin, and Elizabeth was well past menopause.

Consolation for Mary's Loss

It should be noted that while many women of the Bible had areas of pain and loss, we see none with Mary at the time of the conception.

Never-the-less, later Mary stands at the cross witnessing the torturous death of her son and Lord.

In Mary's time of loss and pain we see Jesus Himself providing both a consolation and restoration. The Scripture records in John 19: 26-27:

26 When Jesus therefore saw His mother, and the disciple whom He loved standing by, He said to His mother, "Woman, behold your son!" 27 Then He said to the disciple, "Behold your mother!" And from that hour that disciple took her to his own home.

How powerful is this, that while Jesus is dying on the cross, he utters this command to John. In addition to telling his mother, that John will provide her consolation. This relationship based on their kinship with Jesus would now only deepen in their loss. Thus, providing comfort for their grief.

Evidence of Elizabeth's Walk with God

The Scripture records that when Mary went to the home of Zacharias and Elizabeth, *"the babe leaped in her wound.* Imagine the power of the Spirit already in John as a fetus in the womb, causing him to leap in joy. He could feel the presence of Christ from the womb. The Bible tells us in Luke 1:41-:

"And Elizabeth was filled with the Holy Spirit."

42" And she spake out with a loud voice, and said, Blessed art thou among women, and blessed is the fruit of thy womb.

43 And whence is this to me, that the mother of my Lord should come to me?

44 For, lo, as soon as the voice of thy salutation sounded in mine ears, the babe leaped in my womb for joy."

45 And blessed is she that believed: for there shall be a performance of those things which were told her from the Lord.

God is a God of the impossible. He works the biggest miracles when all hope is lost, as in the case of Elizabeth. Moreover, for His purpose in our lives.

6 THE SHUNAMMITE WOMAN

The prophet Elisha is one of the most powerful prophets in the Bible. One of his extraordinary miracles involves the Shunammite woman. Shunem is a town in the tribe of Issachar. It was given to Issachar along with several other bordering cities. Elisha passed through the village regularly.

The Woman Looks After Elisha

A wealthy woman somehow met Elisha and urged him to eat some food. She did more than that, recognizing that Elisha was a holy man of God she urged her husband to make a room for him on their roof. They put up walls, and she set up a bed. She furnished the room with a table, chair, and lamp. Whenever Elisha came to Shuman, he had a room to stay. This no doubt evidenced her walk with God. When she recognized Elisha as a holy man of God, she went out of her way to provide for him the best she could possibly offer.

Elisha Seeks to Reward the Shunammite

Elisha saw all the trouble she had gone through to see to it that he had a place, and most likely she saw to it he had food to eat as well. He wanted to do something for her. She declined his suggestion of his talking to the King on her behalf or the commander of the army. He possibly wanted to help her get a position, but she replied, *"I dwell among my own people."* She did not want to make a move. Elisha really wanted to do something for her. He asked, *"What then is to be done for her?"*

The Shunammite Woman Was Barren

His servant Gehazi told Elisha, "Well, she has no son, and her husband is old." He told Gehazi to call her. She walked in and stood in the doorway, Elisha looked at her and said, *"At this season, about this time next year, you shall embrace a son."* Her response was, *"No, my lord, O man of*

God; do not lie to your servant."

The Shunammite woman was childless and despaired over not being able to have any children. It was obvious that in her pain she had drawn close to God. So much so that she knew when she was in the presence of a holy man. The Shunammite woman went out of her way for him, saw to it he had all his needs met. She also had empathy for Elisha and was concerned over his not having enough food to eat or a place to stay so she took care of his needs.

So great was the Shunammite woman's pain over her barrenness that when Elisha told her she was going to have a son she said, *"Don't lie to me."* Another words she had lived in such despair over being barren that when Elisha tells the Shunammite woman she will have a child she does not believe it. One year later she gives birth to her son. We see here another case of obedience to God and placing him first brings in her life a miracle, a restoration.

The Child Dies

One can only imagine after having given up on ever having a child, and after having waited so long that the Shunammite woman lived in fear of something happening to her son.

2 Kings 4: 18-37 records the account of how her worst fears were realized. One summer day, while the boy went out in the heat to meet his father reaping, he complained of severe head pain. His father told his servant to carry the boy to his mother. He sat on her knees till noon and died in her arms.

Imagine the horror the Shunammite woman felt as the servant carried her sick child to her. At some point he would have gone unconscious. She must have been enveloped in fear for the worst. The Shunammite woman's son died while she held him on her lap.

The Woman's Actions Evidence Her Faith

The Shunammite woman's first action was to take the dead body of her son and go into the man of God's room--Elisha's-- and lay him on his bed.

Notice, she does not put her son in his own crib, or on her bed, but on the man of God's sleeping place. This was symbolic of her faith. The Shunammite woman then calls to her husband to send her a donkey because she is going to the man of God. Her husband must have assumed the boy was okay because she was leaving. He asks her why she is going because it is not the New Moon or the Sabbath. Her husband associates Elisha with the Temple and the Jewish holy days. She tells her husband, "It is well, which is translated as Shalom, which is the Jewish greeting when meeting or departing meaning peace.

The Shunamite woman does not let her husband know that anything is wrong. She is not thinking of him. The minute she gets on the donkey she tells the driver to go fast and not to slow up. She heads to Mount Carmel to the man of God.

Elisha sees her coming from far away, and he knows that she would not be coming unless something were wrong. He said to his servant Gehazi, *"Look, the Shunammite woman!"* Elisha sends his servant to ask if all is well with her husband and child. Elisha knew that she would not come like this unless something terrible had happened. He knew she was in deep distress and told his servant that God hid from him the reason why she was in such distress.

The Trauma of Barrenness Lingers

In her statement to Elisha, we see how the trauma of the Shunammite woman's barrenness still lingered. She stated to Elisha, *"Did I ask a son of my lord? Did I not say, 'Do not deceive me?'"* The word for deceive in the Hebrew means to mislead, lead astray. This was the fear that the Shunammite woman lived with deep down. She had wanted a child so bad that now that she had one, she feared losing him and her worst fear was realized. This statement revealed the depth of the pain of barrenness.

Elisha Raises the Boy from the Dead

Elisha then instructed his servant Gehazi to take Elisha's staff and to hurry to the child stopping for no one. He was to put the staff on the child's face. This bore no results. Upon entering the house Elisha saw that the boy was dead. He shut the door to his room, prayed alone with God and did a most unusual act. He laid on the boy, put his mouth on his mouth, eyes on his eyes, hands on his hands and stretched himself on the child.

God answered Elisha's prayer. Elisha was so full of the Spirit of God that he was able to bring this child back to life through him. Elisha called to his servant to summon the Shunammite and said, *"take your son."* The story concludes: *"Then she went in, and fell at his feet, and bowed herself to the ground, and took up her son, and went out."*

More Loss for The Shunammite Woman

The Shunammite woman appears again in 2 Kings 8: 1-6. Elisha warns her of a coming seven-year famine. He tells her that she and her household must go to another land; anywhere they can find. Without hesitation they go to the cities of the Philistines. In this time, she suffers several losses. Not only must she leave her home and all her family and friends to live in a strange country to have enough food to eat, but during this dark period of her life her husband dies. When the famine is over, the Shunammite woman returns.

The King Restores All That is Hers

As the king is talking with Gehazi he inquired about the great things Elisha had done. As he was telling how he had restored the dead back to life, the Shunammite woman appeared. The passage continues in verse 5-6.

⁵ Now it happened, as he was telling the king how he had restored the dead to life, that there was the woman whose son he had restored to life, appealing to the king for her house and for her land. And Gehazi said, "My lord, O king, this is the woman, and this is her son whom Elisha restored to life." ⁶ And when the king asked the woman, she told him.

So the king appointed a certain officer for her, saying, "Restore all that was hers, and all the proceeds of the field from the day that she left the land until now."

Not only did the King restore to the woman what was hers, but also with interest. Did she receive her husband back? No, but she did receive the home and income on it that she was not expecting. Thus, we see another restoration after loss.

The Shunammite's Trial Brought Restoration

There is another hidden gem in this story. One may ask, why would God allow the Shunammite woman to lose her son and go through that anguish after she has already suffered so much by not being able to have a child for so long?

Notice it was while Elisha's servant Gehazi was telling the king about the miracle of Elisha raising her son from the dead that she entered and appealed to the King. If it had not been for the reverence, he felt for her after hearing of the miracle of her son, he might not have given her land back with interest. Another words, it was the death of her son and his being raised back to life that led to this miracle.

I have had this happen in my own life, those seemingly unanswered prayers that became blessings years later. Trials that hindered me that I later became grateful for because I had no idea what was ahead in life and those hindrances protected me.

7 TRAGIC LIVES-LEAH AND RACHEL

Rachel and Leah were the wives of Jacob, moreover they are the mothers of the twelve tribes of Israel.

Leah and Rachel

Leah and Rachel were sisters, the daughters of Laban, Jacob's uncle. Leah was the older and she was unattractive. Leah's name means weary. The Bible describes her eyes as weak, delicate, which defines as weak of heart. In addition to Leah's lack of beauty she also suffered from some sort of disability. She would not be chosen by any man to be a wife. Meanwhile Jacob falls in love with beautiful

Rachel. She also fell in love with Jacob. Laban makes Jacob agree to work seven years for her. Only on the wedding night, Laban looks after his homely daughter and tricks Jacob. He sneaks Leah in as Jacob's new wife. Laban then makes Jacob serve an additional seven years for Rachel.

Leah-Unattractive and Unloved

Not only did Leah have to suffer with her unattractiveness and disability, but her father had to trick a man into marrying her. She is now unloved in her marriage. God sees her affliction, Genesis 29:31 affirms, *"When the Lord saw that Leah was unloved, He opened her womb:"* God gave Leah children, and with each child she thought that Jacob would finally love her, but he didn't. She had four sons in total and the fourth was Judah.

Rachel-Beautiful and Loved but Barren

Rachel on the other hand was given great beauty. She and Jacob would fall in love with each other, but it would take 14 years before she could know him as her husband. In addition, she had to live with her father's action. In addition, while Rachel had the love of her husband, she was barren. Rachel became envious of Leah who had four boys. In Genesis 30: 1 she stated to Jacob, *"Give me children, or else I die!"* Verse 2 records Jacob's angry response:

² And Jacob's anger was aroused against Rachel, and he said, "Am I in the place of God, who has withheld from you the fruit of the womb?"

Rachel Desperate for Children

Rachel then suggested that Jacob have relations with her maid Bilhah. He did and she bore Rachel and Jacob two sons. In competition with Rachel, when Leah saw that she had stopped bearing children she gave Jacob her maid as a wife who bore him two more sons.

Leah and Rachel's Conflict

Rachel relays the conflict with her sister by stating in Genesis 30:8, *"With great wrestling's I have wrestled with my sister, and indeed I have prevailed." So she called his name Naphtali.* In Hebrew Naphtali means wrestling. One can only imagine how difficult it was for Rachel who had her husband's love but was not able to bear him any children. She burned with envy of her sister's ability to have babies.

Conflict between Leah and Rachel becomes more evident in the story. Especially over Leah's son's mandrakes. In Genesis 30:14- when Rueben found mandrakes and brought them to his mother Leah, Rachel asked for some. Leah replied, *"It is a small matter that you have taken away my husband? Would you take away my son's mandrakes also."*

Rachel agreed to let Leah sleep with Jacob for the mandrakes. The Bible records in verse 16 that as Jacob came out of the field in the evening, Leah went out to meet him. She informed him, *"You must come in to me, for I have surely hired you with my son's mandrakes." And he lay with her that night.*

It should be noted that despite Rachel and Jacob's love for one another, or that Laban deceived Jacob for her, in Leah's view, her father's decision should have overridden any other agreements. She felt that she was Jacob's rightful wife. Based on Leah's statements we can assume that along with Rachel she also had fallen in love with Jacob. Her feelings prevent her from regarding Jacob's position.

God Answers Leah's Prayer

The Bible says that God listened to Leah and she conceived again and bore Jacob a fifth son. In Genesis 30:18 she states, *"God has given me my wages, because I have given my maid to my husband." So she called his name Issachar."* Issachar means there is recompense meaning to make amends for loss or harm suffered, compensate. God opens Leah's womb again and she conceives again a sixth son. Leah states in verse 20-21, *"God has endowed me with a good endowment; now my husband will dwell with me, because I have born him six sons. So she called his name Zebulun.* Afterward she bore a daughter and called her name Dinah.

Leah Fights for Jacob's Love

During Leah's life, she was fighting for the love of her husband she would never receive. Nevertheless, we also see her reliance on God. While He does not give her the love of her husband, he blesses her with many children.

God Answer's Rachel's Prayer For Children

Rachel on the other hand is more beautiful but is also worldly. We see her early on hiding her father's idols under her skirt. She lies to Jacob to protect her idolatry. She becomes envious of her sister for her ability to have children. She looks to Jacob to give her little ones and he corrects her. He is not in the place of God. Her pain is revealed in the statement, *"Give me children, or else I die."* She implies that this is emotionally killing her. We see her suffering from barrenness.

In Genesis 30:22 the Bible states, *"²²Then God remembered Rachel, and God listened to her and opened her womb. ²³And she conceived and bore a son, and said, "God has taken away my reproach." ²⁴So she called his name Joseph, and said, "The LORD shall add to me another son."*

Again, this phrase, *"God has taken away my reproach,"* meaning shame. No longer would she be different, she will be like the other women who bear children. Rachel could not see that God blessed her with beauty. Neither did she express gratitude over having the love of Jacob. She could only focus on what she did not have.

Rachel-Barrenness and Early Death

Rachel got pregnant with her second son, just as she knew God would give her, but she died giving birth to him. As Rachel was dying, she named him Ben-oni which means *"son of my sorrow"* (Genesis 35:18). As the midwife told Rachel that she was dying, most likely from losing too much blood, her final moment of life was one of grief.

Jacob Favors Rachel's Children

Jacob renamed his son Benjamin, which means son of the right hand. This indicates Jacob's behavior during and after the death of his true love. He favored her children over those of Leah, which led to their jealousy of Joseph. We see this when Jacob went to meet Esau and expected serious conflict. He placed his concubines first with their children, Leah second with her children, and Racheal and Joseph with him in the back behind the others (Genesis 33: 2). It should also be noted that after Rachel's death, Reuben Leah's son, slept with Rachel's concubine Bilhah, in anger against his father most likely for his favoritism.

Rachel's Life of Gifts and Tragedy

Rachel's life was of both being gifted with beauty and the love of her life yet tragedy, barrenness, and early death. Yet her son Joseph would rise to become second to Pharaoh, King of Egypt. He would save his family from a great and severe famine. She also reigns as one of the early mothers of Israel.

Leah Never Receives Jacob's Love

Leah on the other hand would never have the love of her husband. For her entire life she would remain in a state of want and be reminded that she was unloved. She would have to witness her sister receive the love she desired. Adding more to her injury, at her sister's death, her husband would mourn Rachel and favor their children over hers. God could not give her the love of Jacob, but he gave her many children for compensation. Leah had seven natural born children and two via her handmaid. One of her children Judah, would be the direct line of Christ which includes King David and Solomon.

We see in both Leah and Rachel's life, pain, conflict, and suffering. We also see God answering prayers and compensating for their losses. Do we see either of them rejoicing always?

8 MORE WOMEN WHO SUFFERED

On the topic of barrenness, which is a form of loss, in the Bible we also see great women who experienced other losses and trauma.

Moses' Mother

Moses mother Jochebed was forced to give up her youngest son for adoption. Pharaoh decreed that the midwives were to kill all the Hebrew boys when they were born. He did this to control the growing population of Israelites in the land of Egypt. Pharaoh believed they might rise against him. Moses mother hid Moses in a basket of bulrushes and set him afloat on the Nile River to preserve his life.

Pharaoh's daughter found Moses floating and adopted him. God made it so that when Pharaoh's daughter sought out a nursing mother that it was Moses's own mother who nursed him.

Forced Adoption

One can only image that pain Jochebed with being forced to give up her son. When we think of Mother's Day, we celebrate the mothers who raise their children. What about those moms who were forced to give up their children to save their lives.

Moses Raised in Pharaoh's Court

It was necessary for Moses to be raised in Pharaoh's court. This prepared him for the great task by God that came much later in his life. This was to go to Pharaoh and request he set the Israelite's free.

Moses would have never been able to get a meeting with Pharaoh if he had not been raised as a grandson of a previous pharaoh. While this was no doubt a major loss and heartbreak for Moses's mother, she trusted God. He knew best and her son Moses is not only one of the greatest of the prophets, but Moses mother made it into the Faith Hall of Fame.

Adoption in the Bible

Who would ever think that even adoption is covered in the Bible? This should give consolation to any woman who had to give their child up and lives with this pain. Not to mention divorced moms who unjustly lose custody of their children. How many cases throughout the world where the children are even taken from their mother due to war? This was more of the case with Jochebed. She hid Moses for three months until she could no longer hide him. She made the ark for him and sent him among the reeds on the riverbed.

A Proper Child

It is not clear if Jochebed made the ark to further hide Moses. Pharaoh had ordered the midwives to throw the babies to their deaths in the Nile. Given no choice she might have put him in the Nile with the best chance of survival for as long as possible. She put him among the reeds where the ark would get caught and not float into the river. The Bible makes it clear that Jochebed's effort was in part because he was an exceptional baby. Most likely Calm, happy, cheerful, and responsive to his parents.

Esther-Orphaned

The book of Esther is an old Testament book that tells of Queen Esther who rescued the Jews from extermination. The story provides the reason for the feast of Purim. This Jewish holiday commemorates the saving of the Jewish people from Haman, an Achaemenid Persian Empire official who was planning to kill the Jews.

Trauma Survivor

Esther was a trauma survivor. Esther 1:7 tells us that Esther was raised by her cousin Mordecai because she lost her mother and father. She was an orphan. Esther 2:7 reads:

"⁷ And Mordecai had brought up Hadassah, that is, Esther, his uncle's daughter, for she had neither father nor mother. The young woman was lovely and beautiful."

When Esther's parents died, Mordecai took her as his own daughter. Esther lived during the time of the Babylonian captivity when

Nebuchadnezzar went into Judah. Her parents most likely were killed in this invasion. In addition, Esther could have witnessed their murder. After such a great loss in her life, which no doubt pained her for years, we saw a great restoration and miracles. This included Mordecai taking up the task of raising Esther. He was a righteous man of God. She could not have gone into a more perfect home.

Bathsheba-Loss of Her Firstborn Child

We also think of Bathsheba who lost her first-born son she had with David. While she never received that son back, she got to experience her second son Solomon become King of Israel. In addition, Bathsheba's son is in the birth line of Christ. This does not even include the pain she suffered by the death of her husband Uriah. Not to mention the conflict in her heart because it was David who caused his death.

Harlots-Rahab and Mary Magdalene

In addition to the above conflicts, losses, and restorations, we also see among the notable women of God, two prostitutes. Rahab the Harlot, who hid the spies of Jericho and whose family was spared when the Israelites invaded and killed all the inhabitants. In addition, Mary Magdalene, who did not flee when Jesus was arrested, and stood at his cross at the crucifixion. She was quick to visit his tomb and was the first person that Jesus appeared to upon resurrecting. She was given the task of informing the disciples.

While prostitution is a sin, the tragedy lies in what leads a woman to that transgression. In addition to the loss of dignity and the shame.

Hebrews 11 Hall of Faith

Many of the women in this book with all their suffering and faith made it into Hebrew's 11: the Bible's Hall of Faith. Thus, we see a pattern that the women of God who were used for divine purposes all had areas of great suffering. In addition, they had a solid walk with God evidenced by their actions in the Scriptures.

Sarah

11 By faith Sarah herself also received strength to conceive seed, and she bore a child when she was past the age, because she judged Him faithful who had *promised. ¹² Therefore from one man, and him as good as dead, were born as many as the stars of the sky in multitude innumerable as the sand which is by the seashore.*

Moses Mother (and Father)

²³ By faith Moses, when he was born, was hidden three months by his parents, because they saw he was a beautiful child; and they were not afraid of the king's command.

Rahab

³⁰ By faith the walls of Jericho fell down after they were encircled for seven days. ³¹ By faith the harlot Rahab did not perish with those who [l] did not believe, when she had received the spies with peace.

The Shunammite Woman (and Martha)

³⁵ Women received their dead raised to life again.

While this pertains to actual death and raising from the dead, it also has a spiritual meaning. How many of us have an unsaved loved one who we pray for their salvation. Areas of our lives that are destroyed, that God can bring life into. The Scripture speaks of God restoring what the canker worm and locusts have eaten (Joel 2:25). God can even restore the desolations in our life *"the ruined cities."*

And they shall rebuild the old ruins,
They shall raise up the former desolations,
And they shall repair the ruined cities,
The desolations of many generations.

For the Shunammite woman God was able to restore what she lost with interest.

God is near to the Brokenhearted

Unlike the church emphasizes, this unrealistic state of constant joy in Christ, the Bible says in Psalm 34:18, *The Lord is near to the brokenhearted and saves the crushed in spirit."* Psalm 147:3 adds, *"He heals the brokenhearted and binds up their wounds."* You can have the joy of the Spirit and still have within you an inner sadness over you loss. The two can coexist, they did in the lives of the women God used for His purpose.

9 ON SUFFERING-JESUS

It is shocking that so many in church misrepresent true Christianity as having joy all the time. Moreover, they hold the brethren to their ridiculous non-Scriptural standards. When Jesus Himself is an example of suffering to be a comfort for us in ours.

Jesus Our Example

Imagine the King of Kings and Lord of Lords came to this earth and died a most brutal, torturous death. What humility to go to the depths of human suffering Himself so that we would not feel alone. He knows our pain, the worst that this world can dish out to us because he has been through it. Betrayed by one of his disciples, He was ridiculed, beaten, shamed and died a most savage death at the hands of men who He reigns over.

Jesus tells us that in the world we will have tribulation. In John 16:33 He states, *"These things I have spoken to you, that in Me you may have peace, "In the world you will have tribulation: but be of good cheer, I have overcome the world."* Jesus said he warned us that we will suffer and the only peace we will have in this world is in Him.

The Cross

In business a good boss does not place himself above his employees but partakes in the very work that he asks them to do. Jesus is like that business owner. He did not expect us to endure the pain and hardships of this life without putting himself through them first.

The cross in essence is multi-faceted and not just a symbol of redemption but also of consolation. The coming Tribulation and the resulting hardships that lead to the Tribulation are even more reason to focus on the cross and the coming kingdom in which all that is evil and sinful will be eradicated.

Whom the World Is Not Worthy

Some in their lives and ministries have known nothing but hardship. The martyr's lives ended at the hands of another. In Hebrews Chapter 11 lists the champions of faith. Verse 13 states that *"they confessed that they were strangers and pilgrims on the earth."* Verse 14 goes on to say that *"they seek a homeland."* Finally verse 16 adds that *"they desire a better, that is a heavenly country."*

The chapter concludes by mentioning the prophets and others who met brutal tortures and deaths. In addition, those who *"wandered about in sheepskins, and goatskins, being destitute, afflicted, tormented—of whom the world was not worthy. They wandered in deserts and mountains, in dens and caves of the earth."*

We think of those greatly blessed with possessions and good things as those who God favors and finds worthy. These things give one self-esteem and make them feel that have done something right in life. God sees it that those who suffer tremendous hardship, afflictions, and loss for the cause of Christ; the world is not worthy of their presence. During the Tribulation, those who suffer through the hardships and endure the Bible will views as the world is not worthy of them and through it all Jesus will be by their sides.

On Joy and Thanksgiving

If Jesus provided us an example by His suffering, why then do Christians insist that in Him we should feel joy all the time. On the contrary 1 Thessalonians 5:16-18 commands, *"Rejoice always, pray continually, give thanks in all circumstances; for this is God's will for you in Christ Jesus."*

Rejoicing means being glad, calmly happy, knowing that God has our best in mind. In addition, that all things work together for our good. By giving thanks we can focus on the things that God has provided and blesses us with versus on our losses.

The Command to Love One Another

Just as we are commanded to rejoice and give thanksgiving, we are also told to love one another. This also does not come naturally, and it is an area that we work towards. Sadly, it is also the most overlooked in the church today. The church has become a country club of married couples and families whose only concern is for their own. The family itself has become a golden calf. Meanwhile the afflicted, the suffering are told they are not living their life right in Christ. How much easier their burdens if the church fulfilled Jesus's command. But these are the last days and they are growing more difficult in all areas. Many who suffer loss or trauma find themselves very alone. This only adds to their suffering.

10 JESUS SAID TO ENDURE

The message to endure and persevere is clear in Scripture. Jesus referring to the Tribulation Saints states in Matthew 24:13: *"But he that shall endure unto the end, the same shall be saved."* Paul in 2 Thessalonians references the tribulations and persecutions that the church experiences. Paul commands in 2 Titus 2:3, *"Thou therefore endure hardness, as a good soldier of Jesus Christ."* Paul referred to himself as enduring all things for the elect's sake (Timothy 2:10). James 5:11 states:

Behold we count them happy which endure. Ye have heard of the patience of Job, and have seen the end of the Lord; that the Lord is very pitiful, and of tender mercy.

Enduring can make you happy at the end

over the fact that despite your difficult circumstances you remained faithful to God. In addition, God's purpose and blessings come clearer into focus.

Offerings by Fire Most Pleasing to God

It becomes evident when reading the books of Moses that the offerings made by fire were the most pleasing to God. This is repeated over and over throughout the Torah. Fire in the Bible has an association with suffering.

The Jews who suffered bondage and beatings in Egypt were said to have escaped *"the iron furnace."* The prophet Daniel's three friends found themselves in the fiery furnace. With them was one like the Son of Man, who was Jesus with them. Again, this is a reference to trials. 1 Peter 4:12 references the *"fiery trials"* that we go through to test us. It is our prayers to God during our most difficult times that are the most pleasing to him. When we totally rely on Him and seek Him. That is right, when our hearts are broken.

The Golden Censer

Revelation 8 talks about the smoke-filled

censor being thrown to the earth. Revelation 8:3-5 records:

__3__ Then another angel, having a golden censer, came and stood at the altar. He was given much incense, that he should offer it with the prayers of all the saints upon the golden altar which was before the throne. __4__ And the smoke of the incense, with the prayers of the saints, ascended before God from the angel's hand. __5__ Then the angel took the censer, filled it with fire from the altar, and threw it to the earth. And there were noises, thunderings, lightnings, and an earthquake.

These prayers of the saints are the offerings made by fire. The many times we seek God in our trials or stay close to Him in our pain. Numbers 15:3 affirms, *"and you make an offering by fire to the LORD, a burnt offering or a sacrifice, to fulfill a vow or as a freewill offering or in your appointed feasts, to make a sweet aroma to the LORD, from the herd or the flock.*

The Coming End of Pain and Suffering

The reason why the angel throws the censor to the ground is it marks the end of this world and we will not have to pray to God we will be with Him. In addition, all the pain and suffering that goes with living this life is now over.

Putting God First

In all your pain and suffering you must always keep God first. As you walk with him and endure and persevere, your life becomes the sweet aroma. We see in the life of Naomi that she accepted the fact that God had made her life bitter, but we see His divine purpose, which included her story in one of the books of the Bible. This is the book of Ruth, named after her daughter in law, who was a gift of restoration for Naomi.

Misconceptions of the Christian Life

We carry too many misconceptions of the Christian life and of life in general. From how we are to approach our pain, to our belief that it should not exist at all. In fact, pain is a part of our existence and should be accepted. Especially when we have experienced loss. Loss if two-fold: both what we in fact lose and what we never have that we expected should have been in our lives. If loss does anything, the pain is so severe that it causes you to realize just how insecure this life really is. You can have something or someone today and it is gone tomorrow. You reprioritize. If anything will unattached you to this world it is loss and suffering.

The Errors of The Prosperity Gospel

Sadly, the false teaching of the prosperity gospel has replaced sound doctrine. The idea that if one is faithful to God He blesses with great prosperity and health. The truth is more that if God is going to use you, you will suffer tribulation. We see this in the lives of the men and women of the Bible. The end of John the Baptist was not one of prosperity: Herod beheaded him. The Apostles also experienced early death. In the case of Rachel, she died while giving birth. She had prayed for children and her conception was an answer to prayer. Yet she died giving birth.

Source of Great Pain

This book clearly has revealed that the great women of the Bible all had a source of pain. We never see their pain go away, as many erroneously teach about the Christian life, but rather as one trusts in God and makes Him first there comes a restoration. In each of the women's lives a replacement came for their loss, though not what they would have expected or what they originally could have hoped. For several it came after their lives ended.

A Modern Example

A powerful Christian woman of our modern time who had a big ministry speaking worldwide, and whose book still reaches people though she died, is Corrie Ten Boom.

Although Corrie had wanted to marry and had a man in mind, he married someone else. She remained unwed. She had her sister, father and brother and a ministry to the disabled. Her life was mundane and predictable. Until World War II.

During the war her family rescued, and hid Jews and she became the head of a nationwide underground to save Jews. Their operation was discovered by the SS. Not only did they raid their home when she was suffering a fever with the flu, but she was beaten and sent to prison into solitary confinement and separated from her family. Of all times for the raid to occur, while she was sick with a high fever, it could not have happened at a worse time for her.

Loss of Family - Concentration Camp.

Corrie's father died alone without his family ten days after imprisonment and was laid in an unmarked grave. Corrie and her sister Betsy were sent to Ravensbruck, Hitler's notorious concentration camp for women. Many there were political prisoners.

Gladly the Jews that the Ten Booms hid remained safe and were relocated. This is despite the SS threatening a constant guard on the house. The secret room hiding her safeguarded Jews was never found by the police. They said they would keep watch until they came out. God worked a miracle and protected those who Corrie sacrificed her life to save.

Along with experiencing the horrific conditions, starvations, beatings, murders and degradation, Corrie's sister Betsy, her boon companion died at only 59 years old at the camp. Within days Corrie was released. Yet in all this horror, both remained steadfast to God, witnessed, and taught in the camp and God performed miracles including Corrie's release.

Corrie Ten Boon's Ministry

Betsy had visions that came true of Corrie's ministry after the camps. It was to be their service. Not long after Corrie was free, her brother died, and her nephew was murdered at the Bergen Belsen concentration camp. As Betsy predicted Corrie told her story all over the world. Yet, her worst fears had been realized, not only was she a widow, but she lost every close member of her family including Betsy.

After all of this suffering, in the final five years of her life she suffered two strokes, the first taking her ability to speak and finally leaving her totally paralyzed. Like her mother she would become a prisoner of her own body but would most likely see this as an opportunity for prayer and follow in the steps of her mother.

The Hiding Place

Corrie Ten Boom's book *The Hiding Place* published in 1971 sold well over two million copies. Corrie's ministry still goes forward beyond the grave. Her book is one of the greatest Christian books ever written. In addition, her caregiver wrote a work about the silent years of Corrie Ten Boom and how she was still an inspiration. A happy life? On the contrary, Corrie Ten Boon's life during the war was full of unspeakable hardship and loss after loss. In addition to her fears coming upon her.

In addition, the life Corrie and her sister Betsy still teach valuable lessons. Not to mention God's many miracles during that time. Despite severe hardship Corrie Ten Boom and Betsy maintained their walk with God and the Lord Jesus Christ. Corrie struggled and she makes this clear.

God's Plan for You

You do not know what God has in store for you, or what miracles he will yet perform in your life. When the weight of your sorrows is too great to bear, when God seems distant you must persevere. God will come through for you but not in a way you might expect. If you remain faithful and lean on Him the best you are able given your circumstances, He will provide a restoration, a miracle. For Corrie it was her ministry from her suffering and loss and that she was performing the work Betsy foresaw to millions of people.

God Uses Broken Vessels

Meanwhile do not run from your pain or try to erase it. Pain is a part of this life. Do not let anyone make you feel like you should not feel it or are doing something wrong because you do. Do not let anyone tell you that you should not feel the sadness or pain you feel. God uses broken vessels. The God of the impossible performs the greatest miracles in our life when we are most broken.

To Comfort Another

Because of your pain you will be able to also comfort another who is suffering, which is what Jesus commands. He expects this of us. It because Jesus knows this life is difficult. We need to be there to help one another. Where Jesus cannot be there in the flesh, we are to represent Him. He also stated that all men will know we are His disciples if we love one another (John 13:35).

Our Pain Alters and Humbles Us

We cannot stop life from hitting us hard, but if it teaches us one thing, it is that this earth is not our home anyway. Just when we get too comfortable, we are reminded how painful this life really can be. All trauma and loss redirect us. The initial sting abates in time but leaves us forever changed. Some of the pain is so great we will carry it for the duration of our life. We never eliminate it; we just get around it

Loss Causes Us to Gain in Christ

If your loss or suffering lead you to a saving knowledge of the Lord Jesus Christ it was to your gain. If it drew you into a closer walk with the Lord, it also has become a positive in your life. When you are the weakest you are strong if you stay close to Jesus. Paul had his thorn in the flesh, and it kept him humble. Your pain will do the same as it keeps your humanness ever before you.

Beauty for Ashes

The Bible promises that Christ gives us beauty for ashes and comforts us. Isaiah 61:3-4 states:

"To comfort all who mourn
To console those who mourn in Zion,
To give them beauty for ashes,
The oil of joy for mourning

*The garment of praise for the spirit of heaviness;
That they may be called trees of righteousness,
The planting of the LORD, that He may be glorified."*

This is a power packed passage on what Christ promises to give is in exchange for our suffering. But there is one key.

In Everything Give Thanks

1 Thessalonians 5:18 tells us to *"in everything give thanks, for this is the will of God in Christ Jesus for you."* If there is a key that will help you through your pain it is as you give thanks and look at God's blessings in your life. You will learn to be thankful for things you never appreciated and see that in fact despite your sadness, and all that you have experienced, God is at work in your life. Be thankful for the little things because they are much bigger than you realize.

Just like the women of the Bible, if you stay close to the Lord, He will provide a consolation for your loss. He has certainly done so for mine. In addition to giving me the eyes to see His greater purposes in my own suffering. He will also do the same for you.

ABOUT THE AUTHOR

Erika Grey, author, Bible scholar, commentator, journalist has been a born-again Christian for over 40 years She has written numerous books on Bible Prophecy and made contributions in helping to decode the more difficult forecasts. She has spoken on numerous radio stations including Coast to Coast.

This book is one of a series of short books by Erika Grey intended to be quick reads with important information. Be sure to check out Erika's other titles at www.erikagrey.com.

www.ingramcontent.com/pod-product-compliance
Lightning Source LLC
Chambersburg PA
CBHW050528170426
43201CB00013B/2130